Four Quarters

LANA HECHTMAN AYERS

Four Quarters

an homage to T.S. Eliot's *Four Quartets*

NIGHT RAIN PRESS

Copyright © 2017 Lana Hechtman Ayers.
All rights reserved.

No part of this publication may be reproduced, distributed, or transmitted in any form or by any means whatsoever without written permission from the publisher, except in the case of brief excerpts for critical reviews and articles. All inquiries should be addressed to Night.Rain.Press@gmail.com.

FIRST EDITION

Printed in the United States of America
ISBN 978-0-9970834-6-0

Cataloging Information: 1. Ayers, Lana Hechtman; 2. Contemporary American Poetry; 3. Eliot, T.S.; 4. Four Quartets.

Author Photo: Andrew E. Ayers

Layout/Design/Cover Concept by Tonya Namura
using Cochin

Night Rain Press is an imprint of Night Rain Books.

Night Rain Press
PO Box 445
Tillamook, OR 97141

Contact the author at Night.Rain.Press@gmail.com
or visit her website at http://LanaAyers.com

for A.
who walked with me
through the moongate

"Look up at the sky. Ask yourself, has the sheep eaten the flower or not? And you'll see how everything changes."
—Antoine de Saint Exupéry, *The Little Prince*

"There exists, for everyone, a sentence—a series of words—that has the power to destroy you. Another sentence exists, another series of words, that could heal you. If you're lucky you will get the second, but you can be certain of getting the first."
—Philip K. Dick, *Valis*

FOUR QUARTERS

Contents

Burnt Love
3

East Rockaway
15

Manhattan Island
29

Kenai
43

Acknowledgments
59

About the Author
61

Four Quarters

≈ BURNT LOVE ≈

"Reality doesn't exist until it is chosen."
— Bohr Principle of Complementarity

"The surface glittered out of the heart of light."
— T.S. Eliot, *Burnt Norton*

I

If one truly believes in fate,
then future time can be pre-known
and free will is an oxymoron.
If fate exists then all time pre-exists,
arrives in the present pre-made.
What might have been is an absurdity
nothing less than perpetual impossibility.
What might have been and what has been
are parallel universes that never meet.
My footsteps echo in possibility,
down the path we did not take
toward the viewing bench
we never sat upon
overlooking the lake. My thoughts resonate
with yours, or do they not?
                        But to what end
disturbing the leaves around a solemn space
I cannot say.
            Other possibilities
come to mind. Do we dare go there?
"Quick," urged the park ranger to you, "kiss her, kiss her."
Over the bridge, beneath the moongate,
do we show our vulnerability, follow
the official's decree into our first affection?
There were locals and tourists, indistinguishable
milling about, scuttling over dead leaves
in the autumn chill, the thrilling, crisp air.
And a hungry crow cawed, his answer to
the pungent call of discarded popcorn.
A crosswind rose, and the maples
had the look of trees tired of being photographed.
We were the trees' guests, inattentive and attentive,

so moved by the formal pattern branches made,
a complex maze cast upon the lake,
a Minotaur detention center where down meant drowning,
choked with algae, green-tinged.
And the lake was filled with corridors out of shadow.
And what seemed a lily pad rose ineffably, ineffably
gleaming with love-sick frog light.
And there you and I were, reflected, caught in that maze.
Then a cloud passed, and the vision erased.
"Go," said the park ranger, for it had begun to hail,
suddenly, exuberantly, with bough-breaking ferocity.
"Go, go, go," the official said: populace
mustn't witness mystical occurrences.
Time past and time to come,
the kiss we took and the kiss not taken,
lead to limitless transient nows.

II

Oh, T.S., my foggy, boggy mind's
a cloudy junkyard weather that
with what odd broke parts it finds
sings above its unhealing scars
appealing not to deafmute stars
circling profoundly above earth
but to man's claustrophobic dance.
Configured with its abhorrent wars
since the first garden debacle, that
time your God unleashed us, that
paradise was said lost; but a dance
of chance and passionate intention,
I believe, along with bold abandon,
result in utter non-random human
love that reconciles an end to wars.

   At the unstill point of the orbiting universe. Neither
      mass nor massless.
Neither particle nor wave, at the unstill point there is
      always some chance,
neither both trajectory and location, but do not call it
      happenstance
where past and future are indeterminate. Neither up
      nor down,
neither strong nor weak. Probable superstring, the
      unstill point,
there would be no chance and there is always a chance.
I can only say, here is an electron, but not where it has
      been.
And I cannot say, where next, for that is to give it space
      time.
Subatomic freedom effectuates what we know of desire,

the release from stagnation into action, release from
    ultimate
and time-strained quantification, yet imbued
with sensational grace, a quality of being still yet moving.
Bohr complementarity with no observer.
With nonlocality, a whole new whole world
and the old, classical model, outmoded.
The complication of quantum solipsism excites
and repulses the Schrödinger's cat lover in us all.
Unstill, the unpredictability of past and future
is the warp and weave of a sustaining cosmos
engendering life from the stardust void
out of which our flesh emerged.
                                      Time past and time future
engage all of our consciousness.
To be conscious is to be aware of time's
unnatural nature, so a moment at lake's edge,
a moment beneath a gate at sunset,
the first moment our lips met, wind tolling leaves,
are part of the now and future now, in the human
mind where time is made and mined.

III

Here is a place of deep affection
time prior and time since
drain paler. Neither moonlight
softening edges with phosphor flux
transforming starkness into lovely flow
with low light denoting sensuality
nor brilliant sunshine to brighten the soul
brimming the senses with bounty
mud-bathing in nature everlasting.
Neither mass nor energy. A bonfire
in the eyes of a fresh-faced freshman
in love with love with loving him
filled with exuberance, empty of experience
excitement without containment.
Onlookers bristled, tousled by the breeze
of arrival, departure, arrival
winds in and out of aroused breathing
time prior and time since.
Two healthy youngsters holding hands
on the A-train platform, swept away
transported by the wave of passion that breaks
across all five boroughs, Brooklyn, Queens, the Bronx
Manhattan and Staten Island too, even the outer reaches
Westchester, Long Island, and inner-city Newark. Here.
Here in fluorescent glow, in this bustling underground
   world.

  Submerge, submerge further
into the world of incessant togetherness
world within a world that is its own world,
compulsory intimacy, circumspect
and scrupulous with all belongings
surfeit to the world of sense

fodder for the world of possibility
ignition of the world of the spirit;
This is one dimension, and the other
is the same, not in absence of breadth
but in breath and breathing; unstill each dimension rides
on desire, O, on its tunneled ways,
all time prior and time since.

IV

Sun and birdsong have awakened the day,
pale blue skies that wash stars away.
Will the dog lick our faces, will the puss
jump up, into our laps, baby of fur,
nuzzle and purr?

   Steamy
wisps of fresh-brewed coffee curl
up to us? After the shower's massaging spray
has answered skin to skin, and we're clean, unstill.
At the unstill source of this stirring world.

V

Light travels, wind travels
over distance, but that which is merely matter
can be converted. Light after emission reaches
across time. Both by frequency, by wavelength
can light or air currents reach
the unstillness as a tree is unstill
photosynthesizing steadily within its stillness.
Also the unstillness of the star, while wished upon,
that, as well as the wisher, the consanguinity.
Or say that gravity bends time and space,
and beginnings and endings coil around
so beginning and ending become nonlinear.
And all is always arriving. Light waves
bend and sometimes break, intercepted by
glass, liquids, other waves, reflection, refraction,
precise absorption, yet always light moves
at a perceived constant velocity. Stray particles
of dust, water droplets in the atmosphere
always assail them. The light in the Basilica
is most assaulted by fixed dark panes,
archaic shadows beneath its oppressive dome,
the echoing reverberation of patriarchal tomes.

   The vigor of any system is change,
as in I Ching's sixty-four hexagram arrangement.
Wholeness is in itself broken
not in itself whole.
Brokenness is not totality
but rather a degree of openness,
timeless dance of Yin and Yang
bound to the aspect of desire
without limits or limitation

between knowing and unknowing.
Sudden throng of hailstones
even as the sun shines
there rises the unheeded voice
"kiss her, kiss her"
quick now, at last now or never—
ridiculous sad waste of love
spanning past to ever after.

EAST ROCKAWAY

"I keep my ideals, because in spite of everything
I still believe that people are really good at heart."
—Anne Frank

'Home is where one starts from.'
—T.S. Eliot, *East Coker*

I

Where I started is not where I'll end. A succession
of selves, pre-verbal, pre-school, then defined
by school, the early awkward digits, the gawky teens,
the ungainly college and young adult years constrained
by love, contained by new love, stained with lost love,
trained by lost love to gain new love, to maintain love
which is akin to restraining the earth from turning.
Flinting from humankind, young and older
love burns and burns out: there is a time for yearning
and a time for grieving, for solitude's blues
and a time for moonlight to slide between shut blinds
and for sunlight to rut chaste blood again
and for strutting in strumpet winds, passion renewed.

   Where I started is not where I'll end. Now the sun rises
over the wild sea, illumining a thoroughfare
uncluttered by vessels, glittery in the early day,
where you loll on a sandy spot as a white gull wheels,
and the thoroughfare hails you to sail along it
toward light's windblown face, in cool dawn
enthralled. This high tide, there's low fetch,
the crests and swells are gentled.
Silver salmon swim in slackened sound.
The cormorant is close at hand.
                                      Over that wild sea
if you keep your eyes wide, if you keep your ears tuned,
one summer morn, you will hark calypso music
piping playfully from prodigious speakers
and see gleeful revelers on the promenade
of a great contraption of a sailing vessel
borne for pleasure in paradise.
In what many would call undignified display

pairs and triads and odder configurations
hand in hand, arm in arm, grabbing one another
to dance the rhythms, round and round the deck.
Leaping past lifeboats, they form a conga line
with asynchronous high-kicks, boisterous laughter
clumsy hops and colliding stops
their sea legs new and wobbly, lifted in mirth.
Mirth in spite of those left behind on land
punching the clocks. Becoming free,
free in the rhythm of their dancing
living as they do not in their daily lives
free on the high sea under the wide sky
free to drink and dine to excess
free to couple and copulate
free as beasts. Finger snapping, toe tapping.
Feasting and frolicking. Hi-jinx and hangovers.

   Dusk comes, and another night
readies for secrets and sleep. Back on land dusk winds
blow in and in. I am here,
you there, or elsewhere. In our distant nows.

II

How can this late late April
wear the disguise of fall
leaves reddening on the branch
temps more like pre-March
the trillium tipped with frost
white petals freezing over white
early buds wasted by late blight?
Gusting winds' blustery gusts
recall the thirties' storm of dust
when dreamers lost their trust
in the American dream, lives
beset by poverty, hunger, strife
families plowed under in loss.
Now, we're inheriting the curse
of global warming's dire sequel
the pole's deep ice core melting
the rest of us heading for immolation.

   I keep trying to find a way to say it—and keep failing:
a direct inflection in inventive yet conventional verse
leading to the reader's immediate recognition of having
spoken her own words. That poetry is as essential as
    breathing.
It is (to emphasize) what is most often missing.
What is the use of looking forward to a long life
without poetry, with good health and long retirement
in a culture that values only youth? Are we deceiving
ourselves, as we warehouse our frail elders
in nursing homes, Medicare footing the bill for deceit?
Our complacency is an ineffectual denial too,
for who among us will not soon be white-haired
beneath the dye, crow-footed around the eyes

before Botox takes up our lies. There is, it seems to me,
inestimable value in and need of
the knowledge accrued from experience.
This knowledge is poetry in patterns that clarify
the missteps of mankind throughout history
and show opportunities for growth so that
we may be better than we've been. Destroy deceit
by reversing the pressure to stay forever young.
In the middle of your middle age, take comfort
that more life is yet to come, your later, freer years
perhaps aboard a cruise ship sailing off to balmy climes.
And there amid the pulsating beat, disco lights,
risk enchantment. Do not preach to me about the latest
plastic surgery procedure, but rather of its stupidity.
Let us teach one another to strive for self-acceptance,
love ourselves as nature ages us, and love each other.
The greatest wisdom we can hope to acquire
is the wisdom of love: love is regenerative.

   The great ship has set a course for discovery.

   The revelers revel from light to light.

III

O *Dayanu. Dayanu, Dayanu*. It would suffice.
Were there only the potential-filled void and not the
    universe.
Were there only the universe and not our Milky Way.
    Dayanu.
Were there only this solar system and not our earth. It
    would suffice.
Were there only our terra firma, and not the seas, rivers,
    and lakes.
Were there only the waters and not the creatures of the
    waters. *Dayanu*.
Were there only the water dwellers and not the creatures
    of the land.
Were there only the land dwellers and not ourselves, it
    would suffice.
Some great unknowable force is the source of all being
energy binds and entwines us to all in some inscrutable way
string theory cannot be proven by math nor mind but by
    intuition.
I say to my being, be unstill, let energy move through me
which shall be the energy of all potential. Imagine we are
    out in space
and somehow we can see protons spontaneously flash into
    existence.
Angels could be this: a spark in the dark, photon emitted as
    proton is born.
The panorama of the universe is as expansive as the human
    mind
even as our fathomable ocean's onyx abyss that we view
    through
our own inventiveness' inventions, though darker than
    man's first night

on earth. Picture the earliest homo sapiens strolling in
    the scorching
white equatorial light, enjoying a day of plenty when
    finally the sun
lunges over the edge and plunges all into blackness, the
    fear, yes,
but the awe, the imagination spurred as never before to
    wonder.
I say to my being, be unstill, go ardently with awe
for awe inspires goodness and most of all love
for love is the love of all things, and if there is fate
then fate is the sum of love and awe and thrives in
    unstillness.
Go ardently with thought, for thought gives birth to
    kindness.
So darkness shall birth light, and the unstillness, all else.
Soundless shush of meteor shower, and lightning bug.
The white buffalo unseen and the seaside rose.
The prompting at the moongate enticed ecstasy,
not impossible, but requiring vulnerability, opening to
    risk
of loss and gain.

                I keep trying to say something,
something I don't quite have words for. I will try again.
May I find adequate words. In order to be who you are,
who you are meant to be, you must ascertain who you
    are not.
  You could uncover this in a way that may cause
      anguish.
In order to discover what you truly know
    you should entertain the notion of not knowing.
In order to learn all that you can do well
    you should discern what you are ill-suited for.

In order to be your most accomplished self
 you must allow yourself the possibility of failure.
And what you do not know, is nothing compared to
 what you will know.
And what you are ill-suited for is paltry compared to
 your accomplishments.
And who you are is a progression of all the whos you
 are becoming.

IV

On battlefields where flesh preys on flesh
surgeons ply their steel for a momentary
cure, merely sealing in the blood and guts
briefly, success as much chance as art.
For healing, deeper attention in needed.

  Were the necessity for peace heeded
this earth would not be a sacristy
of nuclear and advanced barbaric weaponry.
Mankind is not inherently a breed
of hostility and brokenness.

  Worse, the nursemaid sun and janitor
moon loom beautifully ineffectual to
resolve this mess. No. The answer lies
not elsewhere but in ourselves. In the desert
a man with a beard is not to be feared, but loved.

  Overwhelmed by pain and grief, and for
our kingdom's gain, we name an enemy with our
primitive brain. We have been this way before,
lost holy wars, declared victory. Let hell on earth
be no more. Deploy not weapons, but our best selves.

  No blood sacrifice will ever be drink enough.
We thirst for something clearer. Look to Mother
Teresa, Gandhi, and Martin Luther King, agents
of compassion, fearless dedication. These wise three
we call saints of human grace, the core of goodness.

V

So here I am, middle-aged, enduring more than twenty
    years—
twenty years largely wasted, being at war with myself,
writing and rewriting to find out what's true
and in each new draft, making the same mistakes
unable to attain the perfect words to gain the precise sense
of the one thing I've been attempting to say,
unhaltingly for as long as I can recall. And so each trial
is a journey into futility, a faltering distressing quest
despite the new computer I've wrangled to assist,
a formidable mess of imprecision of thought
and untranslatable emotions. And what I can relate
by simile and metaphor are statements seen before,
so as to be boring or clichéd. True poems imbue the reader
with newness and spur her into passionate action.
Here is my endeavor, to say what still needs saying,
what has not been lost but is not yet found. Despite past
disappointment, I must remain optimistic, even idealistic,
trusting there is no defeat in trying, only success in doing.

    Innocence is where one starts from. As we age
the world becomes less strange, the design more discernable,
an interconnectedness. Not the solitary individual
indivisible, with no attachment to others,
but invisible energy fields teeming through everyone
and not on earth only, but hitching the entire universe,
everything we know, to everything we don't know.
There is a time for going out on the town
and a time for spending the evening at home
(an evening devouring *Leaves of Grass*).
Love is most closely itself
when every moment matters equally.

The young ought to take time to contemplate
that here and now is essential
to build upon the next and the next
into a healthier opportunity
for deeper union, intense community
with the bright earth and dark potential void,
electromagnetic waves, energetic winds, dynamic ocean
this improbable universe. Where I'll end is not where I
    started.

MANHATTAN ISLAND

"Time is a storm in which we are all lost."
—William Carlos Williams

"And right action is freedom
From past and future also."
—T.S. Eliot, *The Dry Salvages*

I

I do not know much about vortices; but surely Manhattan
has an underground energy vortex — strong and volatile,
innervating to enormous degree, unfeasible to prove or
    record,
a charged source, a magnetized force drawing people
    toward it.
A problem only of how to accommodate the masses
    moving in,
a problem solved by building up and up, accepted as
    normal
by the dwellers swelling the island — however, ever the
    vortex fluxes.
In the summer seasons, as temperatures rise so do tempers,
flashing as the heat bellows. The vortex flares unnoticed
by walkers, subway and bus commuters, all the while
    working
its coercive rhythms, in the boardrooms and bedrooms, on
    the docks,
in the parks and restaurants, even in heavenly St. Patrick's
    Cathedral
where incense burns and jeweled stained glass smolders,
in the flickering light of prayer votives.

   The vortex suffuses us, the island circumscribes us;
Manhattan is stalagmite, its buildings and bridges
    transfigure
the sky into which it reaches, the heavens where it launches
signals of this civilization to any other creation out there:
radio stations of talk and rock, soul, cool blues, classical;
television networks of news, sitcoms, dramas, reality shows
that are all more extreme than mundane.
It sends up our wars and woes, the fallen
men, and shattered towers, the battered grail

of misguided faith, broken promises. The island has
    many voices,
false gods and many voices.
                              The moon rests on rooftops.
Seagulls roost on steeples.
                        The island growl
and the island howl are different voices
sometimes heard at once: the throng of conversing crowds,
the catcalls, the rattle of jackhammers breaking into
    concrete
like weak teeth; and the warble of pigeons, the rhythms
of street musicians and the low rumble of the subway
are all Manhattan voices, and the blaring horns
of taxis on their way, and the lit billboard ads
of Times Square: heavenward in downtown smog
the towers
rising, urging us to look up, hardly noticed by
rushing waves of pedestrians, ensconced
in brain-fogs of internal schedules, logged by
watches, laptops, cell phones, anxious
lists worrying present moment into the future,
trying to keep on top of the heap, keep it from toppling,
"too many irons in the fire," "too many balls in the air,"
from before daybreak, well past rush hour, time
a flow whose velocity is seemingly increasing, though
time is measured in manmade beats, restrictive intervals;
digital clocks, wall calendars, step counts,
before
the fall.

II

When will there be an end to it, the smoke trailing,
the exploded tenancy, the imploded cavity,
twin towers collapsing in on themselves, perpetual falling;
when will there be an end to all the ashen wreckage,
the hope of flesh leaping through air, the hopelessness
of their final leap of faith?

   There is no end, but accession, the failing
rescue operations for hours and hours for days,
while emotions were driven to stupefaction,
newness of living among the breakage
of what was assumed as unbreakable, everlasting —
and therefore worthy of faith.

   There is the advancing accession, the assailing
blame of innocence, where radicalism is blameworthy,
fervent devotees of doctrine, the cruelest sort,
all semblance of human compassion unassuaged
by the surety of religious righteousness,
zealots unquestioning in their faith.

   Where is the end to us, our "superior" prevailing
super-power, failing to acknowledge the necessity
for self-examination? We dare not think of a time before
our voice reached across continents, global brokering
of assets, limited resources, with a sense of security
the future was in *our* hands akin to faith.

   We will forever see those images, people leaping
from smoldering upper floors, camera-slowed gravity
pretending possible safe passage, etching instead

the horror of it, the flames and the fall, footage
of loved ones who would never, could never
be saved, not even by the sturdiest faith.

    There is no end to it, the feverish wailings
of agony, the miseries exacted by piety's depravity,
enduring destruction history forges timeless,
ever-drifting drift of smoke and ash, the fuselage
and wings of those two angels of death, that unmade
that which was once prayable, undid the last of faith.

    It seems as civilization progresses,
the architecture of the future regresses, a recursive
consequence of the past, through impassioned fallacy,
encouraged by superficial notions of supreme being,
becoming for populations, a means of disowning the future.
Condemned centuries, the sense of wrongness —
prejudice, bondage, inequality, aggression,
even the utterance of hateful words, all kinds of violence.
In our ignorance, we missed every lesson.
One lesson learned and our ignorance would be undone,
and from its undoing, a new blueprint emerge whereby
we could have evolved. I have said before
that our actions in the present serve as lessons
not for ourselves and one another only,
but for the many generations —who'll remember
us most not for our negligible good deeds,
but our backwards notion of self-assurance
in primacy, not even half looking back
over our shoulders at primitive terrors we
invoked. Let us comprehend how complacency
(whether or not due to dogma,
having failed to do right or feared to do right
is a fault) causes permanent damage

with such permanence as time has. This lesson
now is only apprehended as shameless agony
inflicted by anyone besides ourselves.
Our own future rides the currents of all these actions,
including the injury we inflict but are blind to,
unwarranted and unatoned by prior attrition.
If people remain the same, agonies multiply.
Time is healing, time is redemptive.
Like the river of kindness that flowed where towers rose,
food drives and scholarship funds,
the saying of the names the flames felled that day,
waves of compassion rose to smote the embers,
searchlights beaconed skyward, sweeping remembrance
of tragedy that is a benchmark for our kind
to set a just course by, after febrile centuries
of pious fury, a level course as never before.

III

I can't stop thinking about what Confucius said —
among his many wisdoms, that penetrating one:
Before you embark on a journey of revenge, first dig two graves.
Is there any regret that precedes actions one should come
    to regret?
Revenge seems to succeed regret in the dictionary only.
And the only glory is not in never falling, but in rising when we do.
Such tragedies are hard to move through, but this alone is
    true:
Time is healer. The dead will not be risen, but the living
    must.
While the planes were boarding, the passengers found
    spaces for
their belongings, then settled into their designated places
(those who saw them off at the airport went on their ways
    home),
faces relaxed from rush to relief. Passengers readying
    themselves
for liftoff with chewing gum, thumbing magazines, sending
    emails.
Go gentle, dear fearless travelers. You are leaving your
    future behind
for what comes after this life, no one knows but those
    already gone.
You will never arrive at your intended destinations
you will not arrive at any terminus alive.
While the engines made contrails in the sky behind you,
chosen men in the front cabins waited their holy missions
watching heaven's distance undulate and lessen before
    them.
You did not think of the present as eternal

or the future as past.
At midmorning, in the engines and over the wings,
is the presence of a descending fate (though not foretold
or forewarned so that it might have been unmade).
Go gentle, dear fearless travelers, you are not going
    anywhere known.
You will not be landing at the planned gate,
you will not be met by friends, make the meeting, head
    home.
Between boarding and disembarking, you reach a farther
    shore.
Time as we know it, will be withdrawn, your future
and your past equivalent at last.
At the moment which is neither death nor life,
may you receive some final reprieve from
whatever burdens you carried.
Your death made history, and that event
(though death is common to all)
may come to better the fate of others
who make good the lessons to be taken.
Fare gentle,
        O victims, O office workers,
you who went to work faithfully as any Tuesday,
you who boarded planes that piety turned missiles,
whatever your destination in this inscrutable universe,
let the words of Confucius bear fruit:
And the only glory is not in never falling,
        but in rising when we do.
Go gentle, dear fearless journeyers.

IV

Lady of the harbor, whose torch enlightens,
watch over those who move above you, those
whose business has to do with flight, and
those who travel to places far from their homes
and those who pilot them.

Lady Liberty watch over all those
whose families and friends, whose loved ones
set forth never to be returned to them,
tempest-tossed,
lift your lamp also for them.

Lady of the harbor, lift your lamp on behalf of
those whose planes did not land softly, whose voyages
ended in flames and ashes, who Earth took in pieces,
whose voices shall not be heard on land or sea,
ungolden silence.

V

To investigate the universe, converse with Aristotle,
whose insistence on wholeness misled astronomers
and mathematicians for centuries, or go knock on the door
of poor Copernicus whose heliocentric system shook
the robed ones in Rome to the core. Or have a face to face
(but do not race) with Zeno, so keen on proving
    continuity
of motion impossible. Be discreet if you should meet
Godël for he'll talk your ear off about the fundamental
incompleteness of any set. Let us not forget Newton,
who may or may not have been snoozing under
an apple tree when he came to understand that attraction
and action operating over a distance is the very stuff
of gravity. Yet, sadly, the mechanics of the universe may
not be mechanical at all. When one examines the very
    small,
sub-atomic world, abandon all intuition ye who enter
    there.
Nothing is logical or even predictable though mankind's
curiosity wishes it so, and clings to the notion of certainty.
But to apprehend the intersection of the macro with the
    micro,
the infinitely large with the infinitesimally small is a job for
someone called to quantum physics, not an occupation
    either,
but obsession, wonder and disbelief, and requiring an
    entire
lifetime of surrender to the selfless pursuit of perhaps.
For most of us, there is no way even to imagine Einstein's
space-time, to conceive the warpable weave of the cosmos,
or the duality of light, leaving as a wave arriving as a
    particle,

the wild world unseen, a fermion gang of quirky quarks,
a mass of massless bosons, and a sextet of tasteful
   leptons.
A writhing world we'll never see with our eyes at all
but can only theorize and hope. Only calculated guesses,
tropes followed by dispute and ponderous new guesses.
In science, observation, experiment, careful measurement,
and knowledge only go so far. The rest is imagination.
Here hypothesized *branes* unite
matter and energy that is actual.
Here space and time
are reconciled as one.
The void no empty place —
it brims with potential energy
so that the nothingness is
itself a source of something
charged. And energy is matter
in another state, throughout time.
For most of us, the universe
will remain sublime mystery.
We are only defeated
by not using our hearts
as well as our minds.
Time is the fire
(though none conceive the rate of its flow)
in which we all burn.

KENAI

"It was almost time for lunch. Pain is human."
—Wallace Stevens

"This is the use of memory:
For liberation—not less of love but expanding…"
—T.S. Eliot, *Little Gidding*

I

Late winter here is protracted spring,
nearly eight hours of light and less sodden
a progressive period, subarctic to subtropic
The short day's humming bulb is bright halo,
a calciminer sun that freshens snow and roads,
in refracted air that lights the heart's radiance.
Reflections off the animated river
a tinsel scintillation all afternoon.
And air glitters more than glass or mirror
invigorates the listless mood; milder glacial breeze
in this brightening season. Between freeze and melt
the body's blood quickens. A trace earthy scent
the scent of life awakening. It remains winter
on the calendar though now the bunchberry
is greened with premature growth
of leaves, a process paternally slow
as summer when it erupts in bloom.
This is not nature's primal scheme.
Is this global warming, unstoppable
Nuclear Summer?

                      If you came this way
taking a route you would be less likely to take
from a place you would be less likely to come from,
if you came this way on winter solstice, you'd find
    bunchberry
bare and white, with a spare grace.
It would be a different grace if you arrived later.
If you arrived at dawn like a poet philosopher,
if you arrived at dusk knowing what you wanted,
it would be different, when your plane set down
and you left the blue air up where it was with your

faith in thrust. And what you didn't know you came for
is the translucency, a lust for clarity.
From which the aspiration arises only for breathing
it all in. Whether you had prior ambition
or not, your passion has moved beyond inspiration,
fulfillment alters desire. There are other places
you could end up, some in sunnier climes,
near Tahoe, or Orlando, or even New York —
but the dearest place in time
is here and now.

                             If you came this way,
taking some alternate route, starting from elsewhere,
at some other time, in any other season,
it would always be different: you would need to open
your senses and mind.   You are here for experience,
to enlighten yourself, feed curiosity,
expand yourself. You are here to feel
where glaciers have been. And glaciers are more
than a core foundation of geography, they are ancestry
of human kind, traversing the earth, remaking the land
as so much life died off, sanctioning new life.
The air must have been glassine then, profound
    soundlessness
without the breathing and the breath of species gone
    extinct.
Here, the transversal of epochs and the present
in North America and everywhere. Momentary and
    eternal.

II

Dust that settles out of air on jars
is dust of the past, the dust of stars.
All the elements we know on earth
came from a pre-existing dearth
of matter, no water, no salt, no cells,
a cloud of potential and not much else:
suddenly nucleosynthesis occurs
    making possible all of us.

  We call this hypothesis of course,
though there is evidence to reinforce
by looking back in time with the Hubble
telescope and other devices, a bubble
as some claim, a mother singularity
of intense dense pressure and energy,
expanding cosmic stuff that originates
    our history and fate.

  Eons have elapsed in the universe.
Whether its future is charm or curse
to mankind cannot fully be known,
and whether or not we're on our own
out here, or there are other beings
in other galaxies like the wellspring
we have on this planet, a treasure trove
    of breath and life and love.

In an uncertain hour of the night
    near the end of an interminable dream
    where I was lost in an unending maze
a pallid magpie with a fractious *ay ay ay*
    dragged his shadow across the moon
    on his way to alight in the crabapple tree

free of leaves that made no sound in the frigid breeze.
    Where the passage forked, an achromatic figure
    appeared to me from a loitering lamppost,
blowing toward, lighter than a person should be,
    light as a feather, undulating in wind.
    And I looked upon the upturned face,
that openness and hope with which we might approach
    someone for directions in a foreign town
    and saw a familiar visage (not T.S. as I'd supposed)
another notable I'd never known being born too late,
    but recall
    for the features closely resembling hers
    especially around the eyes, perhaps a composite specter
both actual and wholly uncertain.
    When I collected my courage to speak
    I heard another voice say, "I looked for you before,"
although I was not her, she was not me,
    we were not of one mind, I was still me —
    Her face filling in and the words sufficed
for me to guess who she must be, and so I nodded,
    and so in the cold, I huddled closer, threaded
    her arm through mine, to be more companionable.
At a second fork in the way, the choice
    was needed, go back or forward
    and she steered us for the latter without hesitation.
Frustrated at not knowing what to say,
    I stuttered, "It is such an honor to meet you,
    I would love to know your mind."
And she uttered a sigh. "My good company should
    satisfy. Nor will I recite that
    which you can acquire in books.
Those words well serve their purpose. Let them be.
    And so be it with yours. Forgive the lack
    and luster. What do the blustering bees taste

in December's buds? They taste the coming spring.
    And so we must invent new words and find
    new ways of saying what our voices haven't said.
This urgency for connection, its compassion
    finds no hindrance in my current lack
    of blood and bones. I feel rather at home
with you in this non-material dream dimension,
    a place I never thought of visiting before
    but perhaps now I am, I'll do so more.
We share a passion for language and language
    helps us to know ourselves and others,
    to know what we know and what we do not know.
Let me disclose to you the wisdom of my Fly buzz days:
    Do no harm, and that is a lifetime's work.
    Fan your passions 'til they ignite,
follow your enchantments though others brand
    you foolish. Sweet is the taste of cherished fruits.
    Let not age dissuade you from engagement.
Anger is the mind's contagion, that infects the flesh;
    do all you can to flush it out, lest it rots
    your health as well as all your joy.
And this most of all, do not turn down your reason,
    let your thinking mind prevent the shame
    of sheepish normalcy. Be not blind to vile motives,
to the evil inflicted by supplication to
    chapter and verse of so-called virtuous text.
    Question. Resolve to be your honest best intention.
Claim the honor of being a perceptive being.
    Breathe truth as you would breathe in pure air —
    Truth produces a rare refining measure —"
As I opened my lungs to inhale her accrued wisdom
    (somehow I felt more substantial) day was breaking
    and she faded away into the peal of an automobile
        alarm.

III

According to the respiratory therapist, there are three
    types of
breathers that differ completely, but can occur in the same
    family.
There are the nose breathers, the mouth breathers, and
    those
who breathe using both nose and mouth to varying degrees.
Nose breathers are closest to death, sleepwalking, never
questioning, believing everything, following rules to the
    letter.
Mouth breathers cherish experience, tend to be illicit risk
    takers,
have short memories, flitter from job to job, lover to lover.
Combination breathers love beyond desire, more deeply,
experience a sense of liberation from the past by
    acknowledging
the mistakes of the past, and altering their actions
    accordingly.
They take educated guesses, calculated risks, endeavor
to maturely answer consequences. They look to the future,
though the future may be worse, they breathe in all life —
the faces, the places, the trappings, with an openness,
a willingness for adaptation, evolutional self-renewal.
We are born in innocence,
not yet polluted by life's hypocrisies
and mostly we recover and are well.
When I think about the towers
and the people, mostly good people
who were largely strangers, T.S.,
but all of whom were born innocent
and touched by a common meanness of life,

united and divided by terror.
I think of air travelers at mid-morning,
and of the hundreds up high in their workplaces,
and the rescuers who would not be rescued,
and of other losses all over this world
and of my love who died quietly one night.
Why should we mourn these dead and gone
more than we celebrate those living and breathing?
It is not to try to set the clock back to before loss,
nor is it an attempt to keep time still
so no new losses will be foisted upon us.
We simply cannot stop loving.
Absence does not impede love's flow
like a remembered song into the future.
All who we loved and all who they loved
and all who loved them also
are bound by love's pervasive nature
though existence be discrete.
What love we bequeath to others
has a long history of ancestors.
What love we pass down is a banner
that outlasts death, T.S.
Touched by the indifference of life
we recover and are well.
Love is its own reward, its only motive,
in the air of our dying and breathing.

IV

A raven ascending smooths the air
with a sweep of graceful fervor,
movements many may despair
as an omen of impending terror.
They will resort to organized prayer.
    Others see nothing there to abate,
    redeemed by free will from fate.

    Why such superstition? Enmity.
A need to create enemies to oppose
to prove one's own righteous purity;
greed that proclaims one faith all-knowing,
one truth pursuing a perfect afterlife eternity.
    Better to love life alive, without dictate,
    better to revel in free will over fate.

V

Sometimes things end before they truly begin.
Sometimes endings lead to new beginnings.
For believers in fate, the end is where one begins.
And every breath (every exhalation, moves one
closer to that end which is already slated,
though not known, and every breath feels restrained
somewhat) is tethered to the end from the beginning.
However, breath is also voice and voice is freedom,
for not even the expert speaker can put into words
all the emotions and experiences she has.
Every expression is a beginning and an end,
every poem a birth and a death. And every action
rolls the dice, a breath of life, will it be a sea cruise
to paradise or flight that ends in flames: we take a chance.
We live in the living:
let the breeze blow over us.
We die when we are dead:
the breath of death cannot be unsaid.
The moment in the park and at the towers
are of equal weight. We are people with history
time can redeem, for history is a design
of changing stories. For now, the light holds
on a winter's afternoon, by the sea in a small town.
Our story is now and in the universe.

   Call upon the love within you, let love be the voice of
      Humanity.

   May we never cease from opening ourselves;
from the beginning of our opening
we release oppressive doctrines,
add infinite possibility to our lives.
Over a bridge, through the remembered moongate

when the first of love was new to discover
was one of many beginnings
and endings in the wheel of time.
The directive of the park official
amid the profusion of tourists
(so many, so hard to ignore)
but heard, half-obeyed, in the unstillness
of two beating hearts, held breaths.
Quick now, here, now, always —
the condition of endless potential
offering not less than everything.
Regardless of life's hypocrisies, we will evolve.
We will evolve and be extraordinary
when hope and faith are disentangled
by our capacity for unconditional love
and free will and fate are one.

Acknowledgments & Gratitude

Deep appreciation to the following journals in which excerpts from this collection appear:

The Café Review

Cascadia Review

The Centrifugal Eye

StringTown

Tiger Burning

Sincere thanks to the Helen Riaboff Whiteley Center, especially Arthur Whiteley, Kathy Cowell, and Aimee Urata, for the sanctuary to bring much of this work to fruition.

Eternal gratitude to Ottone "Ricky" Riccio for greeting me at the threshold of poetry and welcoming me in.

Everlasting gratitude to my 3rd grade teacher, Mrs. Sarfaty, for kissing fuchsia lipstick wings
on my cheek and dubbing me a poet.

Profound appreciation to James Bertolino for his generous feedback and friendship.

Endless gratitude to Tonya Namura for her brilliant book design.

Heartfelt thanks to my family of writers and friends, especially the Striped Water Poets, my Kingston critique group, as well as Anita K. Boyle, Jeannine Hall Gailey, Natasha Kochicheril Moni, Nancy Pagh, Linda Warren, and Julene Tripp Weaver. I adore you all.

About the Author

Lana Hechtman Ayers, originally from New York, lives in the Pacific Northwest, where she works as a poetry publisher, facilitates Write Away™ generative writing workshops, leads private salons for book groups, and teaches at writers' conferences. She is obsessed with exotic flavors of ice cream, Little Red Riding Hood, and monochromatic cats and dogs.

Lana earned Bachelor's degrees in Mathematics and Psychology, and holds a Masters in Counseling Therapy, as well as an MFA in Poetry and an MFA in Writing Popular Fiction. A Hedgebrook alumna, Pushcart Prize and National Book Award nominee, she is the author of several collections of poems, including *The Moon's Answer* (2016, Egress Studio Press), *A New Red* (Pecan Grove Press, 2010), *What Big Teeth* (Kissena Park Press, 2010), *Dance From Inside My Bones* (Snake Nation Press, 2007), *Chicken Farmer I Still Love You* (D-N Publishing, 2007), and *Love is a Weed* (Finishing Line Press, 2006). She is currently at work on several speculative novels.

In addition to thriving in the book-loving culture, Lana enjoys the Pacific Northwest's bountiful rain and copious coffee shops. She is a movie addict, a time travel enthusiast, and watches entirely too much Home & Garden television. Her favorite color is the swirl of Van Gogh's *Starry Night*.

www.ingramcontent.com/pod-product-compliance
Lightning Source LLC
Chambersburg PA
CBHW020624300426
44113CB00007B/772